What They Don't Tell You

A Practical Guide for Classroom Management and Teacher Resilience

WALTER CULLIN JR.
&
WYLLYAM HOLLOWAY

Table of Contents

Introduction

Why now? This is the question that we hear a lot regarding why we ventured out to create this small guidebook on building relationships and classroom management. What made you guys go out on a limb to talk about something that has been discussed and presented a million times? Well, the answer for both of us is simple. After spending a considerable amount of our lives in education, over and over we have seen a pattern. We have noticed that the best teachers are the ones who can pivot when things become difficult. They are the ones that can calm down the student who has been deemed "out of control." Not only that, but they have also gotten children to buy into the values and expectations established. Their students are learning as, "The Whole Child." How did those teachers create an environment where students can correct and learn from their mistakes right on the spot and still respond to their teacher appropriately? We feel the answer is simple. Working through a system like we talk about in the next few chapters can assist you in this. Of course, teachers came before us and there will be many after. So, what we are presenting is not rocket science or the next big breakthrough. However, It is paramount to your success, and the advice and strategies help to prevent teacher burnout and fatigue. By investing and reinvesting in these strategies each year, and from class to class, you can no doubt be successful in a long-term (or short-term) teaching career. It will not be easy though, so buckle up. It will be bumpy at times, but you must go through some turbulence to reach clear skies. Ready? Let's Go!

Establishing Norms: Setting the Tone

One of the single most essential elements of being an educator is establishing norms in the classroom. Setting norms within the classroom is essential to curbing unwanted student behaviors. To successfully set norms, you must make a conscious effort to be intentional and consistent. Hold the line and do not be lenient. Leniency will only lead to unwanted problems in the classroom. All the preliminary work that you put in will begin to falter right before your eyes. Furthermore, when setting norms, allow input from your students. Students value the opportunity to be heard and have a stake in what occurs in their learning environment. You can gather student input through surveys, classroom discussions, voting, etc. Once you have agreed upon norms for the classroom, you need to practice them. Students can role play, you can model, and you can also quiz the students. In the beginning, especially the first two weeks of school, hammering the norms is imperative. These two weeks set the tone for the entire year of school. Students may become frustrated with your constant reminders of classroom expectations, but trust that it will be extremely advantageous as the year progresses. As mentioned earlier, setting norms should be one of the two main focuses during the first two weeks of school. Listen carefully! DO NOT do anything academic (curriculum-wise) the first two weeks of school.

Have students work on activities and assignments that allow them to get to know one another. Relationship building activities that allow students the opportunity to familiarize themselves with you and their peers. Some activities to consider are as follows:

- Scavenger Hunt
- 4 Corners
- Rebus Puzzles
- Temperature or Weather Checks
- Trivia
- Would You Rather Questions
- Up/Down

There is a myriad of other activities you can utilize. Whatever you decide, be sure that you engage with your students as they work. There is nothing like a teacher that immerses themselves in the tasks with their students. This is your "in." This is how you begin forging those relationships and building trust with your students. Moreover, norming does not stop in the classroom. There are other places throughout the building in which you must norm. For example, the hallways and bathrooms. Depending on the school's setup and grade, you may have different school-wide procedures for lunch, bathrooms or specials. However, most of the norming for these areas should be similar. In the hallways, the expectation is that the students walk in a straight-line quietly. For middle and high school students, this may look different. Nonetheless, there are some middle schools that require students to be escorted from class to class in a single file line. To ensure student compliance, you must practice these norms. You begin by discussing hallway etiquette in the classroom. Allow students to ask questions and state their thoughts. Acknowledge their questions and concerns while remaining firm on the established expectations. Prior to any transition, students are typically required to line up. Again, for some schools, this is not the case and may look different. For the sake of this book, we will assume that students are required to line up before transitioning. You must have students practice lining up in the classroom first. Watch closely for stragglers and talkative students. Be keenly observant so that you can get an idea of who may need a particular line spot, and who may be a responsible student you can trust. Allowing students to choose their line spot initially is fine. It gives students the opportunity to make a choice and act on their own volition. If a student begins to demonstrate that they cannot handle themselves in a certain spot, then it is time to switch it up. It is important that you explicitly state what will occur if a student cannot handle themselves in line. For example, assigning a student who is having issues in line a particular line spot. Whatever you decide, be sure to stand firm by it and follow through with it.

After practicing lining up, the next focus would be walking the halls as if they are transitioning to lunch or specials. When walking through the halls, stop at different landmarks within the building. This will be your routine stopping points when travelling through the building. Make sure that you can see all your students before proceeding. If students are talking or not in line, do not move along. Wait for full compliance or restart the process all over again. Continue to pause and restart until students are in full compliance. This aids significantly in making sure students are following hallway procedures. Discuss bathroom expectations as a class as well. Inform students how much time they have, the purpose of the bathroom and what will happen if they fail to use it appropriately. Consider a sign-in/sign-out sheet to track bathroom usage frequency. Do not allow students to utilize the bathroom during instruction unless it is an absolute emergency (utilize your discretion). This helps to deter frequent bathroom usage and aids in managing your classroom. You want to minimize distractions and disruptions in an effort to provide quality instruction.

So far, what we have discussed may seem futile, but it certainly pays dividends for teachers throughout the school year. Unfortunately, many academic programs focus heavily on the academia associated with becoming an educator. Lesson planning, educational acronyms and assessments are harped on intensely. Classroom management is discussed superficially. As a result, many new teachers feel overwhelmed and burnout because they are not equipped to manage a classroom. New teachers are taught how to teach students, but not how to manage a classroom and connect to their students. For many, especially those entering urban education, there is a culture shock element associated with teaching. You cannot be an effective educator if you do not understand or make a conscious effort to seek to understand the demographic of children you are serving. In other words, you cannot teach students if you cannot reach them. Point. Blank. Period.

Furthermore, parental relationships are just as important as student relationships. Establish a time for a meet and greet with parents (if your school does not) to get that relationship going as well. Make sure that you have a way to personally reach out to each family to establish a bond between you and each student's parent or guardian. Find out how each parent would like to be contacted and the best times to reach out. You will find that some parents prefer texting, some email and some prefer a call. It is your responsibility to figure this out by connecting with the parents. Additionally, ask the parents if there is a back-up person that you can contact if you are unable to reach them initially. This helps in situations that may spring up that are not anticipated. Contact parents with good news as well as other news. Many parents like to stay informed of behavior, so if they indicate they want this, utilize any time you can to notify them of things they need to know (sleeping in class, excessive talking, will not stay in seat, etc.) so they can be equal stakeholders in the process. If applicable, talk to the previous teacher if the student is returning from the prior school year. The previous teacher typically has information that could be of benefit to you. However, utilize the information cautiously and responsibly. Sometimes one teacher's interaction with a student differs from the next. Therefore, do not allow the opinions of colleagues to dictate how you create relationships with your students.

2

Building Classroom Community

Along with setting norms, you are trying to build the type of environment that all students can agree to and be accountable for. The environment or **Classroom Community** is the governing system for the classroom established by you (As the teacher and lead) and the students of that classroom. This is a contract between you and your class. It is a classroom system that you can both consistently do, under most circumstances. For example, if you have firmly set norms, and have done activities that have fostered opportunities (see **Establishing Norms** section) for the many personalities that you have in your room, then solutions to issues may seem a lot easier to solve. There will always be situations that you haven't encountered much, but even in abnormal cases with your established classroom norms and sense of community, there are still opportunities for academic and social growth. What this allows is an expected system of reward and consequence that all parties deem as fair.

Parts of the Community

Student voice "How Do I Hear Everybody?"

Fostering Relationships

In the first few weeks of setting norms, it is generally fair for teachers to do icebreakers, and get- to- know you type activities. It is during this time you should start to get an idea of who your students are. The purpose of this is multi-faceted. You should get an idea of what type of activities will get most of your students engaged. You will likely also see which students are more outspoken and likely to put themselves out there. The students with the most charisma will likely emerge during this time. Observe if the students with the most influence use that voice positively or negatively. Try to determine your heavy hitters for potential behavioral issues. Watch who gravitates to who and how those relationships affect the environment. If they are not good for the environment, make sure students abide by the expectations set in your norming. The relationship between you and those students will be of great importance. You must try to get to know those students and find common ground. In doing that you must also help those students understand your expectations. Try to establish the best relationship that you can with those students based on fairness and rules you have established. **DO NOT WAIT UNTIL A STUDENT'S VOICE IS LOUDER THAN YOURS!!!!**

As the teacher, you must be the final undisputed voice in your classroom, so no voice can be louder than yours, and even those that are the loudest or most influential must split time sharing their ideas with other students in the classroom. This provides **Equity of Voice**. Also, don't allow students to go home and paint a negative picture of you to the parents. You should have already opened a line of communication with the parent/guardian of your school. Make yourself accessible if issues come up. Parents can be difficult either way, but if you make yourself available to them, then you often can come to workable solutions to issues that may arise.

You should also pay attention to who is a little more reserved during this time. Many of these students do not seem lost or scared, but a little more calculated when they speak for whatever reason. Many students are focused due to what they have been taught within their homes and life experiences. In most situations students will comply because they want to learn and develop the things they are interested in and realize school is the way to do this. There will be days when you are not at your best and students will push you to get back on track. Utilizing these students for the most trusted jobs often motivates these students to work harder. They also like the acknowledgement of their hard work. Compliment them and praise students as much as possible for following expectations and classroom procedures. If you facilitate things correctly, this will happen organically, but remember these students can be at fault at times too and fairness requires that you treat them accordingly in those situations. In many instances, these students will value your relationship and appreciate you holding them accountable.

Finally, you should observe the students who do not seem to lack confidence. They may be into school but lack the skills, or it could be quite the opposite. Helping these students' level up is of extreme importance. To obtain the skills needed academically many of them must go through tailored experiences to gain confidence socially, so proper peer relationships and class atmosphere are of utmost concern. There are many different scenarios here, but for your class that particular year, you should get a sense and feel of who students are during this early formation of community. Your aim is to get an accurate feel for who each student is to create a rule system where every voice in the classroom, (no matter how confident, or indifferent) is heard.

- **TRY This**: Weave icebreakers, projects, and hands-on activities into constant classroom opportunities to have your voice heard and decide on important classroom matters. These are for the rules that are not only reserved for you which you are still working on through the setting of norms (bathroom breaks, walking in lines, classroom noise level, etc.). Online surveys, email contests, polls (whether in-person or hybrid), pro and con conversations, are all ways to do this."

For example, if students like the game 4 corners, you give them four choices to vote on. Students can choose the top four ideas for something like, "How to best decide what will be the classroom reward if students receive 5 compliments for hallway behavior that week." Allow students to go to the corner of the suggestion they like to demonstrate their choice. The corner with the most students wins. In the case of a tiebreaker, the teacher or top student would get to decide. In this case, you have tailored the game by giving suggestions and initiating the challenge but afforded students a choice in how they will be celebrated if they reach the goal. In this example, the consequence of not reaching this goal may simply be not getting the celebration. In other examples, you may have an actual consequence attached to not reaching a milestone or expectation.

- **TIP:** Establish your classroom jobs and rotations for these jobs. Students often value taking part in class in other ways. Classroom jobs can provide the movement, (paper/assignment collector, supply distributor, etc.) and responsibility (bathroom monitor, timekeeper etc.) and prestige (line leader, tech helper) needed to help sustain a well-balanced community. Everyone finds the roles they like the best and is more likely to engage in activities they enjoy.

In all that has been talked about here, your participation in activities and with students is paramount. As was discussed in "Setting Norms," engaging with the students is an important way of understanding how hard you can push students, and where to pull back. It may help you determine what communication barriers you have and how to correct them. This time should help you see how to engage with students when issues arise between you and them. For example, some students will respond to just a look because your relationship is good enough that they can see the social cue and correct the behavior. Some students you cannot just give "the look" to because they need a verbal cue. For example, "Okay Larry, we are not overtalking people. Let us allow Jessica to complete her thought before responding." Other students may need you to stand near them or walk toward them to know that what they have done is not appropriate. Many teachers also utilize discreetly slipping students notes and side conferencing to help issues that arise. It should be able to help you have the conversations (tailored for each individual student) to help students stay encouraged, positive, and on-track. This period is made to help you make the necessary connections with students that will assist you when difficulties arise because difficulties are coming, but also for you to truly exercise the empathy and fairness needed to balance your classroom. Educators ask a lot of students academically. It would be unwise to ignore the social implications caused by the pressures of challenging students in this way. So, it is only right that you treat students as if this is the most crucial time of their lives to develop strategies to resolve high pressured situations, because at the present time and age for them, it often is.

Student accountability: "Buy in To What's Best for the Community."

Once you have gotten a consistent groove with synthesizing your norms with the classroom's norms, you can use the system you established to hold students accountable. Most situations can be resolved within your classroom and do not require the constant use of referring students out to administrators for consequences. If this can be achieved, students will spend most of their designated school time in their assigned classrooms, thus maximizing the time you will have to improve their social and academic standing. Setting Norms and building the classroom community go hand-in-hand for you to get to the point of students subscribing to the discipline system put in place. They will start to remind each other of the incentives and achievements at stake because they have become important to them. Students will also remind each other of proper behavior to avoid consequences. When you teach values like friendship and loyalty students will often try to assist peers in their path to achieve. This may take time, but you continue to go back to what rules and expectations you have established to guide the students in their application of adhering to the rules set. If you consistently do this, your class will be easier to manage and teach.

Disclaimer: Do not get it confused. Only hard work through preparation, patience, flexibility, creativity, and empathy will help you create the environment you want. These words are not meant to give you an effortless way out, but a concrete strategy to form successful classrooms. There is no easy way out. Teaching is extremely hard and can be emotionally draining. It requires, just like anything worth doing, passion and dedication. More importantly, an open-mind and willingness to listen, change, adapt, and adjust.

Increase Patience/Resiliency

"Where's the Calm in my Room?"

In order to increase the patience in your room, you will have to create a space (physically and mentally) for students to feel comfortable. This is good for them, sharing ideas without judgement (with proper scrutiny) and having a space to express themselves in non-verbal ways as well. Having three strikes or zero tolerance rules does not allow for mistakes, which should be welcomed in many cases for "teachable moments" (See **Student Redemption**). Creating this community environment will require some essential elements. Social Emotional Learning or SEL is at the top of almost every school's agenda nowadays and with good reason. The practices of SEL have been correlated to reduce discipline problems when coupled with strong educators who allow appropriate use of these techniques and strategies. An example of this is having strategies for how to communicate nonverbally like hand signals or desk signs could be a way to reduce blurting out in classroom. Also, having a quiet corner in the classroom for a student to process a tricky situation could also reduce temper tantrums and disruptive behavior. This corner can have coloring sheets or puzzles to help a student ground themselves. It could also include a space to journal or draw. Many teachers have specifically designed these areas with couches, throw blankets, rugs, and stress toys.

While others may have exercise balls for students to bounce on and get their excess energy out. Places designated in the classroom may help you keep students in class as opposed to being out of class and disconnected for that time. You will know where your student is, what they are feeling, and how they are calming down. You may have to contact the parents during this time, and you will have a clear explanation as to what is going on. Parents will most likely appreciate this because the student was not whisked away where they are now getting the story second hand from someone else, like a building administrator. As the primary contact of that student, it is your responsibility to know what is happening with your student and to report it to your parents. To ensure this, an environment must be created where you can control as many outcomes as possible. "What makes this work?" you might ask. As the teacher, you must extend the same grace you would want from your supervisor, boss, or principal if you were living up to your institution's standards but was having a tough situation, day, week, etc.

In the moment with students, try to:

Remain Calm: Students will often respond better if your response to them is not yelling, aggressive or over-the top. There will be times when you do need to raise your voice, and even command something with the expectation of it being met right away, but it should be reserved for those times when your leadership will not likely be questioned because you have earned other's respect in this manner.

Pause and reflect: Think back to situations where you felt you needed more understanding when trying to learn something and apply that with students. Having the ability to pivot when something is not working and attempting to show it in a unique way is essential with students who may all need a different road to get there. Taking a deep breath and switching perspectives can be helpful here.

Try to remove personal feelings: Utilizing self-talk, mindfulness, and journaling (*Mark Period Musings* on Amazon is a great journal for teachers) can help you accurately assess how you have done with situations in your class and can lead to a greater realization of problem solving. You must hold yourself to a high standard and be open to criticism of your deficits, even if those criticized are students. If you hear the same thing from students over and over, there is something about your system they still do not get about you. Sometimes this can be solved by fostering better relationships, but reflection of your pedagogy may help you reveal the issue. Speaking with colleagues about situations can be helpful, especially if that colleague has been in the building for a while and seems to have things down or has successfully worked with your current student(s) before. See what they are using that is working. Always being open to this can help add a new wrinkle in your practice.

Use brain and movement breaks. These are vital for students, especially when developmentally the attention span may be lower. Consider the students who are older and may not be provided with many opportunities to move much during academic time. Having opportunities to break and move can alleviate classroom disruptions. It has been shown that students also disrupt when they are bored, so having opportunities for students to go someplace in the room to quell that boredom with something constructive could be helpful. Having a "Mindfulness Minute," break or quick yoga stretch between assignments could also help students stay engaged. Use your creativity to produce something fun and applicable to your students. This also could be an opportunity to try something new for you and your class to bond over.

Student Redemption

"What will allow for the most success?"

In dealing with kids, we often ask ourselves, "When was I the most successful in school?" Quite frequently, the answer is, "When I have felt the most supported." Easy answer, but what does that mean? It means that strong support is conducive for success. Success is facilitated when there's a system in place that is doable with a trustworthy adult who is patient, yet firm. The environment is calm and inviting with only occasional disruptions that do not detract from the learning. Even if a mistake is made, whether behaviorally or academically, it has the potential to be fixed in that moment or setting. Sometimes quickly, sometimes over stretches of time. What's important is that the issue does not always have to result in leaving the classroom. In fact, it rarely should. Refraining from sending students away pays its dividends. You may have to be firm. You may have called parents, but in these kinds of classrooms, students will realize what was fair and where they crossed the line. They will know when a parent call is coming sometimes. But even in those cases, allow students another shot at fixing what they did. This is where you can best benefit children. If you are following the map laid out in this book, you have:

1. Set Norms

2. Built a Positive Classroom Culture

3. Increased Your Patience/Resiliency

Now it is time to extend your system even more by building in ways to fix problems without sending students away. Here is where we use the incidents of misbehavior with assignments that may help them have a greater realization of why these behaviors are intolerable. For example,

A student is being culturally insensitive to a movie being shown about the holocaust. Other students begin to feel uncomfortable with what the students were saying, and it is becoming a disruption to the classroom environment.

What do you do?

A. Send the student to the principal's/vp/ or dean's office

B. Stop class and yell at the student about the importance of culturally respecting others.

C. Talk with the student one on one about his behavior.

D. Call and notify their parents.

While all of these are valid solutions, I would challenge you to be more restorative. In this case, you can provide them with questions about Anti-Semitism, that could be for presentation purposes and provides them with better cultural understanding. This exercise requires students to research, reflect, and try to find valuable ways to pour back into the classroom community. This could be a viable way for students to reinvest when boredom or silliness have taken over.

Below are benefits to using appropriate restorative reflections that will allow them opportunities to redeem themselves:

- Students are given the opportunity to process mistakes and make changes
- Encourages self-reflection and introspection
- Classroom seen as haven (positive classroom culture)
- Deepens trust and relationship with teacher
- Affords students additional learning opportunities
- Reduces punitive responses to behaviors

CHAPTER

5

Conclusion

Warnings & Dangers

This book provides a plethora of practical knowledge and strategies that teachers can utilize to successfully manage classrooms and enhance their pedagogy. However, even if you incorporate these practicalities into your classrooms and teachings, it does not guarantee complete success. As an educator, you must be reflective and willing to adjust when necessary. Amid this pursuit, you will encounter challenges. The challenges can be personal or professional. One of the greatest challenges you will face is exposure to students' traumatic events. As an educator you will hear and become familiar with the troubles that students face. Unfortunately, this could be detrimental to you because it can lead to **secondary traumatic stress**. This comes from you being empathetic towards the students' hardships but limited in your ability to change their situation. Recognizing this early on will be extremely beneficial to your pedagogy and professional career. Vicariously carrying the burdens of your students will prevent you from effectively equipping students with the proper tools to persevere and succeed. This will lead to mental and physical exhaustion and **burnout**. Our aim as educators is to empower students to succeed beyond their unfortunate circumstances. Here are a few tips to aid you in avoiding burnout:

- Exercise

- Ask for help
- Get adequate rest
- Do not take it home with you
- Avoid adopting a "Savior Complex"

APPENDIX A

Definitions

Moral Compass: A sense of what is right, wrong, and how to judge each action accordingly.

A Teacher must create an environment that has a moral compass that their students can agree to and still satisfies or resolves adverse situations in the classroom.

Classroom Community: The culture or tendencies/behaviors of any classroom environment. The Classroom Community is set by the absence or presence of norms set formally by the classroom teacher, or informally by whoever dictates the most influence.

Secondary Traumatic Stress: It is not uncommon for educators who deal with traumatized children to develop their own symptoms of traumatic stress. This is known as secondary traumatic stress.

To best serve their students and maintain their own health, educators must be alert to the signs of secondary traumatic stress in themselves and their coworkers. In a trauma-informed school, staff should be encouraged to practice self-care along with other strategies to guard against or heal from the effects of secondary traumatic stress. Taken from: https://traumaawareschools.org/secondaryStress

Burnout is a state of **emotional, physical, and mental exhaustion caused by excessive and prolonged stress**. It occurs when you feel overwhelmed, emotionally drained, and unable to meet constant demands. Taken from: https://www.helpguide.org/articles/stress/burnout-prevention-and-recovery.htm

Appendix B

Classroom Management Plan Template

Here is a template for you to plan out the first two weeks of your class. These are the routines and systems that students should know when academics start for a seamless (as possible) transition.

Teacher:

Classroom:

Classroom Expectations/Rules:

Classroom Routines:

Morning Routine:

Asking a Question/Talking

Transitions

Going to the Bathroom

Getting out of your seat

Getting Supplies

Class Discussions

When a Student Finishes Early

Visitors in the Classroom

End of the day

Proactive Planning

My plan for positively reinforcing student behavior:

_____

_____

How will I make positive parent contact for students?

_____

_____

What steps will I take when students do not follow classroom expectations?

_____

_____

Where can a student go in my classroom for cool down/recovery?

_____

_____

What will students do while they are in cool down/recovery?

_____

_____

Where can a student go for recovery/cooldown in another classroom?

_____

_____

How will I know they made it where they are supposed to go?

_____

_____

When a student refuses to leave, what will I do first?

_____

_____

How can I give the appearance of calm when I don't feel calm?

_____

_____

How will I communicate with parents when there is a discipline concern?

_____

_____

Example Student Contract

Rules that we agree to commit to:

We will not name call

1. We will be respectful of other classmates when they are talking
2. We agree to be quiet when others are talking.
3. We agree not to laugh at others when presenting.
4. We will try to show understanding during this time of other's conflicts.
5. We agree to make it a safe place for ideas.
6. We agree not to judge.
7. We agree not to share other's information with people who are not in 8A
8. We agree to trust each other with valuable information
9. We agree to take responsibility for the work we are doing.
10. We agree to pay attention.
11. We agree to cooperate and participate during these times
12. We agree to be mature
13. We agree to encourage each other when we are having down moments.

Student name:

_____

Student signature:

_____

Teacher signature:

_____

Sel Reflection Questions for Students

10 What Questions
to Develop a Growth Mindset
in children

1. What did you do today that made you think?

2. What happened today that made you keep on going?

3. What can you learn from this?

4. What mistake did you make that taught you something?

5. What did you try hard at today?

6. What strategy are you going to try now?

7. What will you do to challenge yourself today?

8. What will you do to improve your work?

9. What will you do to improve your talent?

10. What will you do to solve this problem?